# Animals

# Les animaux

lezanee-*moh*

**Illustrated by Clare Beaton**

Illustré par Clare Beaton

b small publishing
BILINGUAL BOOKS

# cat

# le chat

ler shah

# dog

# le chien

ler shee-*yah*

# horse

# le cheval

ler sh-*val*

# COW

# la vache

lah vash

# rabbit

# le lapin

ler lap-*pah*

# sheep

# le mouton

ler moo-*toh*

# goat

# la chèvre

lah shevr'

# chicken

# le poulet

ler poo-*leh*

# mouse

# la souris

lah soo-*ree*

# pig

# le cochon

ler coh-*shoh*

# duck

# le canard

ler can-*ar*

# A simple guide to pronouncing the French words

- Read this guide as naturally as possible, as if it were British English of a generally South-Eastern variety (so-called RP).
- Put stress on the letters in *italics* e.g. lombool-*onss*.
- Don't roll the r at the end of the word, for example in the French word le (the): ler.

| | | |
|---|---|---|
| Les animaux | lezanee-*moh* | **Animals** |
| le chat | ler shah | **cat** |
| le chien | ler shee-*yah* | **dog** |
| le cheval | ler sh-*val* | **horse** |
| la vache | lah vash | **cow** |
| le lapin | ler lap-*pah* | **rabbit** |
| le mouton | ler moo-*toh* | **sheep** |
| la chèvre | lah shevr' | **goat** |
| le poulet | ler poo-*leh* | **chicken** |
| la souris | lah soo-*ree* | **mouse** |
| le cochon | ler coh-*shoh* | **pig** |
| le canard | ler can-*ar* | **duck** |

Published by b small publishing, Pinewood, 3a Coombe Ridings, Kingston-upon-Thames, Surrey KT2 7JT
© b small publishing, 1994
1 2 3 4 5
Design: *Lone Morton*  Editorial: *Catherine Bruzzone*
Colour reproduction by Vimnice International Ltd, Hong Kong  Printed in Hong Kong by Wing King Tong Co. Ltd.
ISBN 1 874735 80 8 (paperback)
ISBN 1 874735 81 6 (hardback)
British Library Cataloguing-in-Publication Data.
A catalogue record for this book is available from the British Library.